Juicing Quiz

W	U	A	A	S	D	J	H	E	Q	L	I	M	E
C	N	F	C	A	R	R	O	T	S	O	Q	U	F
B	P	G	S	P	I	N	A	C	H	N	E	U	D
H	C	Q	P	U	F	E	N	N	E	L	K	L	K
B	T	B	E	E	T	S	E	T	V	B	J	G	N
A	P	P	L	E	Q	G	I	N	G	E	R	Y	X
O	R	A	N	G	E	W	K	A	L	E	U	E	W
S	T	R	A	W	B	E	R	R	I	E	S	D	E
X	P	A	R	S	L	E	Y	C	E	L	E	R	Y
H	V	M	N	V	K	I	Y	W	P	L	O	H	H

Kale
Spinach
Cucumbers
Celery
Apples
Ginger root

6 Carrots
1 Beet
1 Cucumber

Celery
Cucumber
Orange
Parsley
Ginger
Lemon

2 Beets
6 Carrots
2 Stalks of Celery
Lemon

9 Carrots
Spinach or Lettuce
Kale
Lemon

9 Carrots
2 Cucumbers
2 Oranges
Ginger

1 Handful of Kale or Spinach
2 Cucumbers
1 Granny Smith Apple
Lime
Ginger

Grapefruit
Lemon
Oranges
Pineapple

Apples
Celery
Ginger
Lemon
Orange
Spinach

While every precaution has been taken in the preparation of this book, the publisher assumes no responsibility for errors or omissions, or for damages resulting from the use of the information contained herein.

FASTING BOOK FOR HEALTH, FITNESS, WEIGHT LOSS & DETOXING 11 JUICING FOR BEGINNERS RECIPES WITH DELICIOUS & HEALTHY FRUIT & VEGETABLE JUICES

First edition. July 12, 2017.

Copyright © 2017 Juliana Baltimoore.

ISBN: 978-1386479789

Written by Juliana Baltimoore.

My Favorite Quote

"Juices of fruits and vegetables are pure gifts from Mother Nature and the most natural way to heal your body and make yourself whole again." — Farnoosh Brock

Why You Should Read This Book

Why You Should Read This Book Juicing is beneficial to your health, but what if you're looking to juice for a specific health benefit? Find and choose the benefit you're looking to juice for below!

Applying a daily juicing ritual will help with the following:

Weight Loss (I lost 40lbs within a period of 2 month by combining my Secret Morning Elixir, Juicing, Smoothies and a light meal plan)

Antioxidants

Alzheimer's Prevention

Asthma Help (I suffered for years from breathing problems and Asthma and finally was able to get rid of it because of my daily Juicing and Smoothie ritual)

Blood Cleanse

Arthritis Prevention

Bone Protection

Cancer Prevention

Cervical Cancer Prevention

Breast Cancer Prevention

Colon Cancer Prevention

Liver Cancer Prevention

Lung Cancer Prevention

Prostate Cancer Prevention

Cataracts Prevention

Ovarian Cancer Prevention

Stomach Cancer Prevention

Digestion

Detoxification

Energy

Digestion

Heart Disease Prevention

Immune System

Hydration

Improving Eyesight

Improved Complexion

Increased Blood Circulation
Kidney Cleanse
Increased Libido
Liver Cleanse
Lower Blood Pressure
Lower Cholesterol
Macular Degeneration Prevention
Mental Health
Osteoporosis Prevention
Pain Relief
Reduce Inflammation
Reduce Water Retention
Stroke Prevention

More Benefits From Applying A Daily Juicing Habit:

Increase in energy and alertness as well as a renewed sense overall health and vigor

When you lean the art of juicing you can enjoy delicious and freshly made fruit and veggie juices to boost your system

Enjoy drinking morning boosting juices to get your day started and to be ready to face new challenges

Play with all kinds of flavors and combinations of ingredients in order to find the one combination that you simply can not live without anymore

You can say no to sick making preservatives, chemicals, additives, and yes to natural sweeteners and a wonderful flavor experience

Discover all kinds of juices that you can make and use for other things like:

Freezing your own juices for later usage

Use your homemade juices for your own self-made cooking and baking recipes like pies, breads, soups, sauces, muffins, cakes and many other delicious treats

The juice makes an excellent stock or natural source of sweetener and they are much easier for the body to process than refined sugars

When you really put your mind to juicing, I imagine you will be amazed by all the wonderful uses you can find with these magical, healthy and healing juices

Welcome to the wonderful and magical world of juicing!

Introduction

"The word juicing scares people because they think that drinking liquid is dieting. What they don't realize, is that they are regenerating their blood, cells, and organs to live a longer fulfilling life."

Welcome to the wonderful world of juicing!

Thank you for purchasing my juicing book that helped me in association with drinking smoothies which helped me lose 20 pounds over two months.

When I lost my weight I started to juice and blend at the same time. What I did was either juice or blend a couple of times a day and I combined it with eating healthy clean foods for 1 meal and a healthy snack or two throughout the day. I included lots of healthy fibers and protein and avoided fats and sugars.

The more juices and smoothies you drink in combination during the day and the less processed foods you consume the more weight you are going to lose.

After having gone through my first Juicing-Smoothie diet for a period of around 60 days, I was able to lose weight for the first time in my life. Not only did I lose the weight, but I was also able to keep and maintain my weight until today.

I am consuming my juices and smoothies on a daily basis and I have never been feeling more energized, stress free and fit.

I am going to share my experience with juicing in this book.

If your goal is to lose weight in a delicious, healthy, effective, quick, effortless and non-harming way, make sure to consume a combination of juices and smoothie recipes.

This combination is what helped me in the end become successful with my weight loss goal and combining juices and smoothies also provides you with more different types of healthy drink variations.

You can also check out my Smoothies series at the end of the book.

Just one last tip before we get started with the actual recipes.

These healthy ingredients and nutrients that are inside these juices do even become more beneficial to your body and mind if used and consumed in combination with a light yoga workout or any other workout that you prefer.

When I am on a juicing/smoothie diet or when I am maintaining my weight after such a diet, I am always adding some Hatha Yoga poses to my daily schedule. You can use any light workout that you like and enjoy doing in order to accelerate your weight loss in a very natural and healthy way.

Before I had some health issues like breathing problems and asthma, stress and sleeping problems, but since I included daily Yoga combined with these healthy juices and smoothies that I am consuming on a regular basis into my lifestyle, I am a new person.

Feeling sick is an experience of my past.

I am so happy that I got started with changing my lifestyle from a common and unhealthy meal plan to one that includes these delicious and healthy juices which kind of transformed my life into a balanced, healthy, energized and clean lifestyle!

I am enjoying this lifestyle so much that I decided to motivate and encourage others to get started with juicing, too.

Depending on your own goals and preferences, you can either consume juices to become a healthier you or you can apply them as a juicing diet or a combination of juicing and smoothie diet in order to develop a leaner body or to lose some pounds.

Make sure to first consult your doctor or physician to make sure that this diet is a good fit for your own personal situation.

Preparing these healthy juices with pulp does not take much time out of your schedule, and if you'd like to learn some cool time management tricks that apply to a healthy lifestyle that includes disciplines like yoga and/or meditation then I highly recommend my sister's book series that you can find on the marketplace as well.

Each juicing recipe for weight loss includes a list of ingredients that you need to have in order to get started. Each juice does not take longer than 5 minute in terms of preparation.

For each juice recipe, simply follow my 5 Minute 6 Step Juicing System chapter and make sure to use organic products, fruits and vegetables whenever you can.

I include exactly the same recipes that helped me lose 40 lbs over two month. I combined these juicing recipes in combination with my smoothie recipes for weight loss.

I hope you enjoy the book and I hope that you will get lots of inspiration and stimulation out of the book in order to be able to take advantage and be empowered by the fact that you can lose weight very effectively, but also by the fact that these healthy juices are helping you tap into some very powerful health benefits.

Remember, each and every recipe and ingredient has its own benefits for weight loss and health!

All you have to do is identify your goal and take your daily action steps. If you follow my juicing diet model from this book, you will have the same success with these delicious and healthy juices.

If you are looking to just become healthier, make sure to integrate more and more of these juice recipes into your daily meal plan and if you are looking to lose weight, first check with your doctor and then you can follow my juicing for weigh loss recipes.

Everybody has a different goal and you can consume less or more of these juices depending on your personal situation, your goal and your lifestyle.

One thing is for sure, if you get yourself into the habit of consuming these juices, you will empower and transform your body and mind with the result of a healthier, fitter, cleaner and leaner you!

The 5 Minute 6 Step Juicing System

Step by Step Instructions For Juicing

For all these juicing recipe simply follow my 5 minute step by step instructions.

Step 1

Wash all veggies and fruits. Going through this thorough cleaning process will help prevent a nasty food-borne disease. I love to use organic vinegar because it is the most natural and organic solution, buy there are other options available if you prefer using products that are specifically designed for washing vegetables and fruits.

Step 2

Peel and cut all your fruits and veggies. Remember, you are juicing raw vegetables. This is why you need to cut them into small pieces before you get started. Especially if you are applying crunchier fruits and veggies such as carrots. Some high speed or high power juicers or a combination of juicer/blender like the Vitamix are able to take veggies and fruits in their whole form. In this case just follow the manufacturer's manual. Peel the skin of all your veggies and fruits. You also need to peel fruits like apples, melons, bananas, papaya, mango, pineapple, kiwis, bananas, avocados, etc.

Next cut and chop the fruits and veggies such as leafy greens and fruits.

Step 3

Put your fruits and veggies into your favorite juicer or blender or a combination of juicer/blender (Nutribullet) and strictly follow the directions of the manual that comes with your machine. The manual will tell you what buttons to punch and what speed to use.

Juice the softer fruits/textures first.

You will see that when you are juicing the crunchier veggies and fruits they will help you push the softer and more delicate fruits and veggies through the blades.

If you are not using a juicer and only have a blender available, make sure to first strain the juice from citrus fruits like oranges, lemons, grapefruit, etc. When you are finished you can either leave the pulp inside the juice or take it out. It is totally up to your preference.

Next add the juice back to your mixture in the blender and proceed from there.

Step 4:

Juice and blend everything together as per instructions from your manual. You can always add some raw honey or sweetener depending on your goal with these juices. If the juice is too strong for you, you might also add some ice cubes or source water.

I only add ice cubes and water to smoothies, but some friends of mine who got started with juicing told me that some of the juices were too strong for them and they added ice cubes or water. In the summer time, ice cubes might be a refreshing alternative.

You will see that experimenting with your juicing process will help you discover many varieties and alternatives which makes juicing such a fun and exciting experience.

Step 5:

Try a variety of fruit and vegetable mixtures. As you experiment with juicing, you will find many combinations that you will enjoy on a daily basis. Some that pair well include apples with carrots, and leafy greens with kiwi. Try anything you want to taste. Create several go to recipes for yourself that you can use to make a healthy habit out of juicing.

Step 6:

The last step is a very important one if you want to enjoy your juicer/blender for a very long time.

Make sure to clean your machine ASAP and once you are done with your juice.

This helps prevent nasty bacteria growth and in order to prevent any diseases that related to hygiene.

Use warm water and dish soap. You can also use vinegar to clean and then run the pieces through the dishwasher.

If you do not have a dishwahser take extra care with the cleaning process.

Step 7:

Make sure to add lots of fiber to your smoothies, eat whole fruits and veggies throughout the day in order to stay balanced otherwise you might risk a dietary deficiency.

Step 8:

Enjoy your refreshing and delicious juice!

Step 9:

Refer to chapter Juicing For Weight Loss if your only goal is to lose weight with juicing.

Why My Juicing Diet Works

I had to find out a different way to lose weight because no diet worked on me. Finally with these detoxing and fat burning juices that I have created via my juicing weight loss program I was finally able to have success and was able to rebooted my system.

Today I am able to keep off the 40 lbs that I lost with my juicing diet because I am respecting my juicing ritual. It is not hard anymore like it was when I first tried to lose weight.

Here is my lemon elixir that I drink every morning before I have my first juice.

Ingredients:
1 cup of warm or room temperature source water
Juice from 1 lemon (organic if possible)
1 teaspoon of raw apple cider vinegar
A pinch of cinnamon
1 teaspoon of raw honey (alternatively you can also use a couple drops of stevia)

For example, you can use stevia if you are on a yeast cleansing diet or low sugar diet.

I drink this every morning, whether I am "feasting" or not, this is my morning coffee and I enjoy my morning elixir ritual!

What this morning elixir ritual does for you:
This morning elixir stimulates digestion and it releases toxins from the liver. It also jump starts your digestive enzymes.
Benefits of this morning lemon elixir ritual:
Raw honey benefits:

* Raw honey is loaded with minerals, vitamins & enzymes

* It helps cleanse your liver, flushes out fat from your body when done first thing in the morning on an empty stomach and remove toxins

* Raw honey soothes indigestion (it relieves acidity in your stomach)

* Energy booster

* Anti-microbial and anti-fungal

* Raw honey helps to keep your skin clear (it helps with skin conditions such as ring-worms, eczema & psoriasis)

Apple Cider benefits:

* Apple Cider is a natural remedy for heartburn
* It can help clear up your skin conditions and acne
* It promotes digestion and apple cider will keep you regular
* Apple cider helps control weight
* It can help regulate your blood sugar
* Apple Cider helps reduce sinus infections and sore throats
* It is very rich in potassium and enzymes
* It can help ease menstrual cramps
* It also helps promote youthful healthy bodies and skin

Lemon benefits:

* Lemon helps make the body more alkaline (increases pH)

* It provides lots of Vitamin C

* It purifies your blood and detoxes you

* Lemon is a cleansing agent & tonic for your liver by helping it produce more bile

Powerful Beginner Juice

If you are a beginner in juicing this one is what you should get started with.

Pouring the contents of delightful oranges and green fruits and veggies into my favorite blender (in my case I am using the Nutribullet because it juices and keeps the pulp in the glass plus it also makes my favorite smoothies) and whipping everything together into a zesty healthy green elixir is what I loved most when I got started with juicing. The experience of making these healthy delights is unmatched and it got me very excited and involved when I first got started with juicing.

This zesty Powerful Beginner's Juice contains the following ingredients:

Ingredients:
Apples - 3 medium and preferably organic (3" dia)
Celery - 4 stalks, large and preferably organic (11"-12" long)
Fresh Ginger - 1/4 thumb (1" dia)
Lemon organic (with rind if organic) - 1/2 fruit (2-1/8" dia)
Orange (for juicing and peeled) - 1 large (3-1/16" dia)

Spinach - 5 cups and organic if possible

Directions:

For the directions please refer to the chapter where I am talking about my 5 Minute 6 Step Juicing System.

Here is a short instruction that sums up what to do. Make sure to refer back to my 6 step process for juicing so that you get the whole idea of juicing.

In this case peel the apples, ginger, lemon if not organic and orange.

Next cut and chop the fruits and veggies.

Put all the fruits and veggies from the ingredients list into your favorite juicer or blender or a combination of juicer/blender (Nutribullet) and strictly follow the directions of the manual that comes with your machine.

The manual will tell you what buttons to punch and what speed to use.

Juice the softer fruits/textures first.

You will see that when you are juicing the crunchier veggies and fruits they will help you push the softer and more delicate fruits and veggies through the blades.

If you are not using a juicer and only have a blender available, make sure to first strain the juice from the lemon and orange.

Once it is finished you can either leave the pulp inside or take it out. This is totally up to your preference.

In this case you have to add the juice back to the blender and proceed from there.

Juice and Blend the juices with the other ingredients together as per instructions.

You can always add some raw honey or sweetener depending on your goal with these juices. If the juice is too strong for you, you might also add some ice cubes or source water.

Enjoy your refreshing and delicious Powerful Beginner's Juice!

Citrus Immunity Booster

This is my secret citrus beauty juice and I make sure to mix it into my daily meal plan because it helped me control my Asthma and breathing problems.

The secret combination of grapefruit, lemon and oranges is what makes this juice a Vitamin C booster.

It is a is also a great liver detoxifier.

In a condition of insufficient oxygen and breathing problems (mountain climbing, etc.) lemons are very helpful.

I suffered from Asthma and breathing problems and have been able to get rid of it by changing by eating and drinking habits. Drinking this juice is part of my daily juicing ritual.

Vitamin C in lemons for example helps the body to neutralize free radicals that are linked to most types of diseases and aging.

This Citrus Immunity Booster is a winner and it contains the following ingredients:

Ingredients:

1 Grapefruit, organic if possible and peeled
1 Lemon (organic if possible and you can keep the rind if organic)
3 Oranges (juicing oranges and peeled)
1 large slice of pineapple (preferably fresh or canned)

Directions:

For the directions please refer to the chapter where I am talking about my 5 Minute 6 Step Juicing System.

Here is a short instruction that sums up what to do. Make sure to refer back to my 6 step process for juicing so that you get the whole idea of juicing.

In this case peel the grapefruit, the lemon, the oranges and the pineapple.

Next cut and chop the fruits.

Put your fruits into your favorite juicer or blender or a combination of juicer/blender (Nutribullet) and strictly follow the directions of the manual that comes with your machine.

The manual will tell you what buttons to punch and what speed to use.

Juice the softer fruits/textures first.

You will see that when you are juicing the crunchier veggies and fruits they will help you push the softer and more delicate fruits and veggies through the blades.

If you are not using a juicer and only have a blender available, make sure to first strain the juice from the oranges, grapefruit and lemon.

Once it is finished you can either leave the pulp inside or take it out. This is totally up to your preference.

In this case you have to add the juices back to the blender and proceed from there.

Juice and Blend the juices with the pineapple together as per instructions.

You can always add some raw honey or sweetener depending on your goal with these juices. If the juice is too strong for you, you might also add some ice cubes or source water.

Enjoy your refreshing and delicious juice!

Everyday Go To Juice

A combination of healthy and lean making kale and spinach is what this smoothie is all about. The Everyday Go To Juice is a perfect solution if your goal is to follow a lean and clean juicing diet.

So what is so beneficial about the Everyday Go To Juice power booster?

The secret ingredient of Kale. Kale contains a rich source of antioxidant related health benefits. It also contains glucosinolates which provide the body with cancer preventive benefits.

Kale also provides you with detox activating isothiocyanates and cardiovascular support.

I have tested this juice with a lot of friends and family members before adding it to my favorite collection of juices. They all got some great benefits out of drinking this Everyday Go To Juice on a daily basis.

I am constantly testing and proving new juicing recipes that I am gradually adding to my "Tested & Proven Juicing Recipe Collection"

This one has passed the test because it is not only delicious, but it is such a healthy treat and perfect for you if you are trying to lose weight with juices.

Spinach, kale and celery might not sound appealing to you at first, but the combination of all the ingredients is turning this juice into an absolute winner. It does not only taste deliciously, but it provides your body and brain with a powerful mix of rejuvenating and healing nutrition.

This Everyday Go To Juice drink contains the following ingredients:

Ingredients:

1 large handful of organic spinach and organic kale (if you do not have both available just use one of them)

1 bunch of celery (organic if possible)

3 cucumbers (organic if possible)

8 carrots (organic if possible)

2 green apples (organic if possible)

2 oranges (juicing oranges)

1/2 inch ginger

Directions:

For the directions please refer to the chapter where I am talking about my 5 Minute 6 Step Juicing System.

Here is a short instruction that sums up what to do. Make sure to refer back to my 6 step process for juicing so that you get the whole idea of juicing.

In this case peel the cucumbers, carrots, apples, oranges and ginger.

Next cut and chop the fruits and veggies.

Put all the fruits and veggies from the ingredients list into your favorite juicer or blender or a combination of juicer/blender (Nutribullet) and strictly follow the directions of the manual that comes with your machine.

The manual will tell you what buttons to punch and what speed to use.

Juice the softer fruits/textures first.

You will see that when you are juicing the crunchier veggies and fruits they will help you push the softer and more delicate fruits and veggies through the blades.

If you are not using a juicer and only have a blender available, make sure to first strain the juice from the oranges.

Once it is finished you can either leave the pulp inside or take it out. This is totally up to your preference.

In this case you have to add the juice back to the blender and proceed from there.

Juice and Blend the juices with the other ingredients together as per instructions.

You can always add some raw honey or sweetener depending on your goal with these juices. If the juice is too strong for you, you might also add some ice cubes or source water.

Green Beauty Juice

This is my secret green beauty juice and I make sure to mix it into my daily meal plan because I enjoy the beautifying benefits of it. It really makes my skin soft, hydrated and wrinkle free. I add some powerful organic and self-made beauty products for my skin care and this is all I need to stay beautiful from the inside out.

I am working on a new series where I divulge my skin care and beauty secrets and you can soon check them out and add them to your home spa and beauty program, too.

A combination of juices and smoothies, the benefits from my self- made beauty and skin care system and a light yoga and meditation workout is all I need in order to create the ultimate healthy lifestyle for myself and my family.

The green beauty juice is a fortified and nutritious combination of healthy and lean making superfood greens like kale, cucumbers and spinach.

Mixing nutritious veggies like kale and spinach and fruits like apples and lime will bring a sweat taste to this juice because fruits help neutralize strong and bitter flavors that might come from the veggies.

The ginger gives this juice drink some powerful health benefits like immune boosting actions.

The reason kale is becoming popular is because it helps you fill up without a lot of calories to speak of. It doesn't have any fat, has plenty of fiber as well as iron and Vitamin K. Because of its antioxidant content you'll get anti-inflammatory benefits which helps to reduce the symptoms of inflammation, while also helping to avoid the rise of certain diseases. It also helps to restore and maintain an alkaline state.

This Green Beauty Juice contains the following ingredients:

Ingredients:
1 handful of either Kale or Spinach (organic if possible)
2 cucumbers (organic if possible)
1 apple (granny smiths are the best because I have tried out everything)
1/2 Lime (organic if possible)
1/4" ginger

Directions:
For all these For the directions please refer to the chapter where I am talking about my 5 Minute 6 Step Juicing System.

Here is a short instruction that sums up what to do. Make sure to refer back to my 6 step process for juicing so that you get the whole idea of juicing.

In this case peel the cucumbers, apple, lime and ginger.

Next cut and chop the fruits and veggies.

Put all the fruits and veggies from the ingredients list into your favorite juicer or blender or a combination of juicer/blender (Nutribullet) and strictly follow the directions of the manual that comes with your machine.

The manual will tell you what buttons to puch and what speed to use.

Juice the softer fruits/textures first.

You will see that when you are juicing the crunchier veggies and fruits they will help you push the softer and more delicate fruits and veggies through the blades.

If you are not using a juicer and only have a blender available, make sure to first strain the juice from the lemon.

Once it is finished you can either leave the pulp inside or take it out. This is totally up to your preference.

In this case you have to add the juice back to the blender and proceed from there.

Juice and Blend the juices with the other ingredients from the list above together as per instructions.

You can always add some raw honey or sweetener depending on your goal with these juices. If the juice is too strong for you, you might also add some ice cubes or source water.

Enjoy your refreshing Green Beauty Juice that will beautify you from the inside out!

Orange Eye Health Elixir

If you love tasty juices with some powerful orange ingredients that are super healthy for your eye sight and taste deliciously, then you might consider the Orange Eye Health Elixir.

Carrots have a rich supply of antioxidant nutrients called beta carotene. Carrots will supply your body with antioxidant benefits, cardiovascular benefits and they boost your visions health.

Pouring the contents of a delightful oranges, cucumbers, carrots and ginger into your favorite blender (in my case I am using the Nutribullet because I love its versatility) and whip it all together into a zesty elixir that heals and keeps your eyes healthy.

This zesty Orange Eye Elixir contains the following ingredients:
Ingredients:
9 carrots (organic is best)
2 cucumbers (organic is best)

2 fresh juice oranges

1"ginger (the secret ingredient)

Directions:

For the directions please refer to the chapter where I am talking about my 5 Minute 6 Step Juicing System.

Here is a short instruction that sums up what to do. Make sure to refer back to my 6 step process for juicing so that you get the whole idea of juicing.

In this case peel the cucumbers, carrots, oranges and ginger.

Next cut and chop the fruits and veggies.

Put all the fruits and veggies from the ingredients list into your favorite juicer or blender or a combination of juicer/blender (Nutribullet) and strictly follow the directions of the manual that comes with your machine.

The manual will tell you what buttons to punch and what speed to use.

Juice the softer fruits/textures first.

You will see that when you are juicing the crunchier veggies and fruits they will help you push the softer and more delicate fruits and veggies through the blades.

If you are not using a juicer and only have a blender available, make sure to first strain the juice from the oranges.

Once it is finished you can either leave the pulp inside or take it out. This is totally up to your preference.

In this case you have to add the juice back to the blender and proceed from there.

Juice and Blend the juices with the other ingredients from the list above together as per instructions.

You can always add some raw honey or sweetener depending on your goal with these juices. If the juice is too strong for you, you might also add some ice cubes or source water.

Enjoy your refreshing Orange Eye Health Elixir that will beautify you from the inside out!

Detoxifying Juice

Who says that vegetables are for lunch and dinner only? This leafy green and lean cocktail contains delicious and zesty fruits that are swirled into the greens and this smoothie makes for a perfect wholesome and healthy start of your day so that you do not need to wait for lunchtime to eat these healthy veggies.

It does not only taste deliciously, but kale provides the body with anti-inflammatory health benefits. The Vitamin C of the lemon detoxifies your body and destroy intestinal worms and the carrots are helping your eye sight. Just to name a few health benefits that come with this detoxifying drink.

This Detoxifying Juice contains the following ingredients:

Ingredients:
9 Carrots (organic if possible)
1 large handful of organic spinach or lettuce of your preference
1 large handful of kale (organic if possible)
1 lemon (organic if possible)
Directions:

For the directions please refer to the chapter where I am talking about my 5 Minute 6 Step Juicing System.

Here is a short instruction that sums up what to do. Make sure to refer back to my 6 step process for juicing so that you get the whole idea of juicing.

In this case peel the carrots and lemon.

Next cut and chop the fruits and veggies.

Put all the fruits and veggies from the ingredients list into your favorite juicer or blender or a combination of juicer/blender (Nutribullet) and strictly follow the directions of the manual that comes with your machine.

The manual will tell you what buttons to punch and what speed to use.

Juice the softer fruits/textures first.

You will see that when you are juicing the crunchier veggies and fruits they will help you push the softer and more delicate fruits and veggies through the blades.

If you are not using a juicer and only have a blender available, make sure to first strain the juice from the lemon.

Once it is finished you can either leave the pulp inside or take it out. This is totally up to your preference.

In this case you have to add the juice back to the blender and proceed from there.

Juice and Blend the juices with the other ingredients from the list above together as per instructions.

You can always add some raw honey or sweetener depending on your goal with these juices. If the juice is too strong for you, you might also add some ice cubes or source water.

Enjoy your Detoxifying Juice that will burn the fat and detox your body!

Beet Juice Booster

This is a fortified and nutritious combination of healthy and lean making raw greens like celery and red/orange raw foods such as beets and carrots.

This juice gets its rich flavor from the mix of green red and orange raw foods.

Who says that vegetables are for lunch and dinner only? This lean green cocktail contains delicious and zesty lemon that is swirled into the juice.

This juice makes for a perfect wholesome and healthy start of your day so that you do not need to wait for lunchtime to eat these healthy veggies.

If you feel that the juice is too strong or too bitter, you can always add an juicy apple into the blend to make it sweeter in taste.

I enjoy it with apples as a breakfast juice and without apples as a lunch or dinner option.

The Beet Juice Booster contains the following ingredients:

Ingredients:
2 beets (organic if possible)
6 carrots (organic if possible)

2 stalks of celery (organic if possible)

1/2 lemon (organic if possible)

apples (depending on your own preference and time of the day)

Directions:

For all these juice recipe For the directions please refer to the chapter where I am talking about my 5 Minute 6 Step Juicing System.

Here is a short instruction that sums up what to do. Make sure to refer back to my 6 step process for juicing so that you get the whole idea of juicing.

In this case peel the beets (or buy them already prepared and ready to use), carrots and lemon.

Next cut and chop the fruits and veggies.

Put all the fruits and veggies from the ingredients list into your favorite juicer or blender or a combination of juicer/blender (Nutribullet) and strictly follow the directions of the manual that comes with your machine.

The manual will tell you what buttons to punch and what speed to use.

Juice the softer fruits/textures first.

You will see that when you are juicing the crunchier veggies and fruits they will help you push the softer and more delicate fruits and veggies through the blades.

If you are not using a juicer and only have a blender available, make sure to first strain the juice from the lemon.

Once it is finished you can either leave the pulp inside or take it out. This is totally up to your preference.

In this case you have to add the juice back to the blender and proceed from there.

Juice and Blend the juices with the other ingredients from the list above together as per instructions.

You can always add some raw honey or sweetener depending on your goal with these juices. If the juice is too strong for you, you might also add some ice cubes or source water.

Enjoy your Beet Juice Booster!

Green Orange Breakfast Power Cocktail

The ingredients of this powerful juice are all very beneficial for the body and brain.

Spinach is one of the most nutrient dense packed foods you can provide your body with. It proves you with energy. Spinach helps you fill your stomach without adding a lot of calories and you feel satisfied and full.

Spinach contains phytonutrients that are working as antioxidants battling against the free radical damage.

By consuming spinach you are helping to nourish your body on a cellular level.

Spinach is a great ingredients for weight loss juices.

Spinach is also an alkaline powerhouse. Baby spinach is great, too. Since there are so many other alkalizing vegetables out there, I recommend trying out different variations and concoct a juice that will send your pH levels to the sky.

This is also the reason why I love combining spinach and kale or baby spinach with spinach and kale.

The health benefits of celery are very powerful, too. In addition to being an alkaline food, celery is very low in calories and it is a great weight loss ingredient for juicing if weight loss is on your mind.

Celery is a great combination as a third ingredient because it brings even more health benefits to the table.

I always love to add celery into fruit based juices as well because it adds a bit of spiciness without overshadowing the sweet flavors of the fruits.

Experimenting with and knowing the benefits of all these ingredients is key to a successful juicing experience.

Parsley is the third green raw ingredient that powers up this juice drink to the next level. Parsley also helps keep your body alkaline. This green herb is not only powering up your juice with lots of health nutrients, but it helps bring out the freshest taste ever. It freshes up the taste of your juice because it adds more vitamins and minerals to your juice.

The great thing is that you can grow your own parsley pretty easily at home and always have it ready to freshen up your juices, smoothies and other recipes that you are making.

I only grow my own parsley and include it in most of my juicing drinks.

The fourth green ingredient of this power packed juice is the cucumber. The cucumber is a heavy hitter. I always keep a good stock of cucumbers at home. Cucumbers are alkaline, and they do contain so much water that it is a very hydrating vegetable.

As you can see this juicing drink is a loaded with powerful greens that you can mix up and find lots of variations that might work for you. I just add some zesty ginger, orange and lemon to this power cocktail which makes the bitter taste of the celery sweeter and perfect for a healthy morning and breakfast juice with a zest.

The Green Orange Breakfast Power Cocktail contains the following ingredients:

Ingredients:
4 Stalks of celery (organic if possible)
1 Cup of Spinach or baby spinach (organic if possible)
2 Cucumber (organic if possible)
1 Orange (organic if possible)
Few sprigs of parsley (organic if possible)

1 small knob of ginger (organic if possible)

1 lemon (organic if possible)

Directions:

For all these juice recipe For the directions please refer to the chapter where I am talking about my 5 Minute 6 Step Juicing System.

Here is a short instruction that sums up what to do. Make sure to refer back to my 6 step process for juicing so that you get the whole idea of juicing.

In this case peel the lemons, limes, carrots, and beet (or buy prepared).

Next cut and chop the fruits and veggies.

Put all the fruits and veggies from the ingredients list into your favorite juicer or blender or a combination of juicer/blender (Nutribullet) and strictly follow the directions of the manual that comes with your machine.

The manual will tell you what buttons to punch and what speed to use.

Juice the softer fruits/textures first.

You will see that when you are juicing the crunchier veggies and fruits they will help you push the softer and more delicate fruits and veggies through the blades.

If you are not using a juicer and only have a blender available, make sure to first strain the juice from the lemon and orange.

Once it is finished you can either leave the pulp inside or take it out. This is totally up to your preference.

In this case you have to add the juice back to the blender and proceed from there.

Juice and Blend the juices with the other ingredients from the list above together as per instructions.

You can always add some raw honey or sweetener depending on your goal with these juices. If the juice is too strong for you, you might also add some ice cubes or source water.

Enjoy your Orange Juice Detoxifier!

Apple Carrot Beet Trianon

If you love tasty juices with some weird secret ingredient combinations that are super healthy and taste deliciously, consider the Apple Carrot Beet Trianon juice elixir.

Pouring the contents of a delightful apple, green and red veggies into your favorite blender and whip it all together into a zesty elixir that will supply your body with a cocktail full of these healthy nutrients is part of my daily juicing ritual.

This zesty Green & Red Health Elixir contains the following ingredients:

Ingredients:
  2 Carrot (organic if possible)
  1 Apple (organic if possible)
  6 Celery Ribs (organic if possible)
  1 Beet (small and organic if possible)
  1 hand full of cilantro and/or parsley and/or cilantro
  1" size slice of ginger (organic if possible)

Directions:

For all these juice recipe For the directions please refer to the chapter where I am talking about my 5 Minute 6 Step Juicing System.

Here is a short instruction that sums up what to do. Make sure to refer back to my 6 step process for juicing so that you get the whole idea of juicing.

In this case peel the beets (or buy them already prepared and ready to use), apple, carrots and ginger.

Next cut and chop the fruits and veggies.

Put all the fruits and veggies from the ingredients list into your favorite juicer or blender or a combination of juicer/blender (Nutribullet) and strictly follow the directions of the manual that comes with your machine.

The manual will tell you what buttons to punch and what speed to use.

Juice the softer fruits/textures first.

You will see that when you are juicing the crunchier veggies and fruits they will help you push the softer and more delicate fruits and veggies through the blades.

Juice and blend all the ingredients from the list above together as per instructions.

You can always add some raw honey or sweetener depending on your goal with these juices. If the juice is too strong for you, you might also add some ice cubes or source water.

Enjoy the Apple Carrot Beet Trianon!

Liver Cleanser Juice

The liver cleanser juice contains a combination of healthy and lean making cucumbers, beets and carrots. This combination is what this juice is all about.

The beets, carrots and cucumber are all nutrient-rich and packed with antioxidants and this is what makes this juice so powerful. This drink is a true immune system booster. It also is a powerful liver cleanse and detox drink because it cleans your system and makes it toxin free.

Beets provide the body with a rich source of Vitamin C and a wide range of other health benefits. The beetroot also contains folate and this helps prevent cancer and heart diseases.

The carrots enhance your vision health. Carrots provide you with a rich supply of antioxidant nutrients called beta carotene.

Cucumbers contain so much water that it is a very hydrating vegetable which combines very well with the healing benefits of the beet and the carrots.

This hydrating Liver Cleanser Juice is the perfect power booster for hot summer days, in the morning and whenever your body needs a good supply of hydration and it contains the following ingredients:

Ingredients:
6 carrots (organic if possible)
1 beet (organic if possible)
1 cucumber (organic if possible)

Directions:
For the directions please refer to the chapter where I am talking about my 5 Minute 6 Step Juicing System.

Here is a short instruction that sums up what to do. Make sure to refer back to my 6 step process for juicing so that you get the whole idea of juicing.

In this case peel the beets (or buy them already prepared and ready to use), carrots and cucumber.

Next cut and chop the veggies.

Put all the veggies from the ingredients list into your favorite juicer or blender or a combination of juicer/blender (Nutribullet) and strictly follow the directions of the manual that comes with your machine.

The manual will tell you what buttons to punch and what speed to use.

Juice the softer veggie textures first. You will see that when you are juicing the crunchier veggies first they will help you push the softer and more delicate ones through the blades.

Juice and Blend all the ingredients from the list above together as per instructions.

Enjoy this refreshing Liver Cleanser Juice!

Beet Strawberry Carrot Empowerer

Let's talk about a powerful combination of some fortified and nutritious red/orange superfoods like carrots, beets, strawberries and green superfoods.

The secret of this juice is the combination of the red/orange superfoods together with the greens.

This is a magical mixture of orange and green nutritious and healing vegetables and fruits. These are ingredients that do not only taste deliciously, but they will also give your body and brain the most powerful health benefits.

Carrots have a rich supply of antioxidant nutrients called beta carotene.

These delicious orange vegetables are the source not only of beta carotene, but also of a wide variety of antioxidants plus other health supporting nutrients.

Other benefits of carrots are antioxidant benefits, cardiovascular benefits and vision for your health.

The real benefit of strawberries is that they are tasting great and that they are providing enough nutrients to the body.

Strawberries provide a boost to your immune system. They helps your eyes and they help fight cancer. They also helps with cholesterol and with inflammation. They also have anti-aging properties.

The mix of greens combined with orange and red raw fruits and veggies is what makes this juice so special.

The Beet Strawberry Carrot Empowerer contains the following ingredients:

Ingredients:

1 beet (organic if possible)
4 carrots (organic if possible)
1 cup of strawberries (organic if possible)
6-8 kale leaves (organic if possible)
3 cucumbers (organic if possible)

Directions:

For all these juice recipe For the directions please refer to the chapter where I am talking about my 5 Minute 6 Step Juicing System.

Here is a short instruction that sums up what to do. Make sure to refer back to my 6 step process for juicing so that you get the whole idea of juicing.

In this case peel the beet (or buy already prepared and ready to use), carrots and cucumbers.

Next cut and chop the fruits and veggies.

Put all the fruits and veggies from the ingredients list into your favorite juicer or blender or a combination of juicer/blender (Nutribullet) and strictly follow the directions of the manual that comes with your machine.

The manual will tell you what buttons to punch and what speed to use.

Juice the softer fruits/textures first.

You will see that when you are juicing the crunchier veggies and fruits they will help you push the softer and more delicate fruits and veggies through the blades.

Juice and Blend all the ingredients from the list above together as per instructions.

You can always add some raw honey or sweetener depending on your goal with these juices. If the juice is too strong for you, you might also add some ice cubes or source water.

Enjoy the delicious Beet Strawberry Carrot Empowerer!

Leefy Green Superfood Immune Booster

Let's talk about a powerful combination of ginger root, celery, spinach, kale, cucumbers and apples.

The secret ingredient of this juice is the ginger root. Let's take a look at what the ginger root can do for you.

The anti-inflammatory properties and active principles of the ginger root are thought to provide pain relief in multiple numbers of ways.

It has the power to stop migraines in their tracks and to ease the aches of arthritis and joint pain.

It also fights ovarian cancer. It seems that ginger has the ability to eliminate the dangerous cancerous ovarian cells. Ginger also seems to slow the progress of bowel cancer.

Ginger also has a boosting effect on the immune system, making you fit and healthy.

Make sure to consume this immune system boosting smoothie drink on a daily basis to stay healthy and clean all year around!

I suggest to drink this juice in slow sips and you can keep it near your workspace so you can take a sip throughout the day.

Ginger also improves your breath. It can cleanse the palate leaving your mouth feeling refreshed.

Ginger protects against nuclear radiation and if you want to get the full benefits of this advantage you will have to consume a daily dose.

Ginger also strengthens your immunity. An improved immune system can mean that you get ill less often. It means that you will recover quicker. It also means that when everyone else around you is coming down with something you can stay fit and healthy.

Ginger also fights cancers. Ginger has been shown to help treat various forms of cancer, including ovarian cancer.

Ginger protects against Alzheimer's disease.

Ginger helps to slow down the loss of brain cells that typically is the precursor to Alzheimer's disease.

Ginger is perfect for weight loss because it stimulates the appetite. If you have a very sluggish digestive system and find out that you need to get your digestive fire going before eating a meal, ginger can help you out.

Ginger can also help as an appetite stimulant to get your digestive juices flowing so that you are better able to digest foods and lose weight as a side effect because improper digestion of food leaves the food fermenting in your digestive system which can lead to weight gain as a side effect.

Ginger is a fat burning superfood and it acts as a fat burner. Ginger helps you feel satisfied and full. This means that you will eat less food which will help reducing your overall caloric intake in the end.

Ginger is a true magical secret ingredient and this juice combines ginger and turns it into an even healthier raw power cocktail.

I am enjoying the benefits of ginger every day. If I do not have enough time to make a juice because I am pressed in time, I consume at least a glass of ginger water or ginger tea with lemon.

If you are looking to lose weight like I did, you make sure to drink a glass of this magical ginger water or ginger/lemon water (cold or hot as herbal tea) throughout the day and in little sips. If you apply this ginger water method you will always feel full and satisfied.

This Leafy Green Super Food Juice contains the following ingredients:

Ingredients:

6 leaves Kale (organic if possible)
2 cups Spinach (organic if possible)
2 Cucumbers (organic if possible)
4 stalks Celery (organic if possible)
2 apples (organic if possible)
1" ginger root (organic if possible)

Directions:

For all these juice recipe For the directions please refer to the chapter where I am talking about my 5 Minute 6 Step Juicing System.

Here is a short instruction that sums up what to do. Make sure to refer back to my 6 step process for juicing so that you get the whole idea of juicing.

In this case peel the cucumbers, apples and ginger.

Next cut and chop the fruits and veggies.

Put all the fruits and veggies from the ingredients list into your favorite juicer or blender or a combination of juicer/blender (Nutribullet) and strictly follow the directions of the manual that comes with your machine.

The manual will tell you what buttons to punch and what speed to use.

Juice the softer fruits/textures first.

You will see that when you are juicing the crunchier veggies and fruits they will help you push the softer and more delicate fruits and veggies through the blades.

Juice and Blend all the ingredients from the list above together as per instructions.

You can always add some raw honey or sweetener depending on your goal with these juices. If the juice is too strong for you, you might also add some ice cubes or source water.

Enjoy this Immune Booster!

Red Kale Juice

The ingredients of the Red Kale Juice are all very beneficial for the body and brain.

The secret combination lies in the mix of red and green ingredients.

The beetroot is one of the most healthy vegetables on earth. Consuming beets will help you feel energized. Beets are great for nourishing your brain. It can assist in lowering blood pressure.

Beets contain a very broad amount of minerals and vitamins. Add some beets to your juices to instantly up and power pack your nutrients without adding more calories or fat. It contains folate and this helps prevent cancer and heart diseases and Magnesium is keeping your energy levels up. It is also a very rich source of Vitamin C.

The alkaline Kale combined with the beets makes an unbeatable juice cocktail that helps you reenergize and rejuvenate at the same time. I enjoy one of these whenever my energy levels are down.

The Red Kale Juice contains the following ingredients:

Ingredients:
1 handful of kale (organic if possible)
2 handful spinach (organic if possible)
6 stalks of celery (organic if possible)
3 spray of parsley (organic if possible)
1 lemon (organic if possible)
1 lime (organic if possible)
½ bulb of fennel (organic if possible)
1 beet (organic if possible)
3 carrots (organic if possible)

Directions:
For all these juice recipe For the directions please refer to the chapter where I am talking about my 5 Minute 6 Step Juicing System.

Here is a short instruction that sums up what to do. Make sure to refer back to my 6 step process for juicing so that you get the whole idea of juicing.

In this case peel the lemons, limes, carrots, and beet (or buy prepared).

Next cut and chop the fruits and veggies.

Put all the fruits and veggies from the ingredients list into your favorite juicer or blender or a combination of juicer/blender (Nutribullet) and strictly follow the directions of the manual that comes with your machine.

The manual will tell you what buttons to punch and what speed to use.

Juice the softer fruits/textures first.

You will see that when you are juicing the crunchier veggies and fruits they will help you push the softer and more delicate fruits and veggies through the blades.

If you are not using a juicer and only have a blender available, make sure to first strain the juice from the lemon and lime.

Once it is finished you can either leave the pulp inside or take it out. This is totally up to your preference.

In this case you have to add the juice back to the blender and proceed from there.

Juice and Blend the juices with the other ingredients from the list above together as per instructions.

You can always add some raw honey or sweetener depending on your goal with these juices. If the juice is too strong for you, you might also add some ice cubes or source water.

Enjoy your Red Kale Juice!

Juicing For Weight Loss

Juicing removes fiber from nutrient dense food. Make sure to include an appropriate amount of fiber rich food in your daily diet plan. Juicing should be a complement to a well-balanced healthy diet, not a complete substitute.

Make sure to eat whole fruits and veggies or drink smoothies with fiber because juicing has the tendency to remove fiber which is an important nutrient. Fiber helps keep the digestion on a balanced level and fiber keeps your cholesterol in control.

Make sure to add lots of fiber to your smoothies, eat whole fruits and veggies throughout the day in order to stay balanced otherwise you might risk a dietary deficiency.

You will find that your appetite finds raw foods more filling. Cooking foods can cause the loss of up to 97 percent of water soluble vitamins A, E, D and K.

Uncooked and raw foods such as juices do contain more vitamins and nutrients. These nutrients are more satisfying to the body which means that the body's metabolism will keep running efficiently. Consuming these juices will keep your weight loss efforts focused and you are going into the right direction.

Juicing also helps kick start the digestive process of the body and enables a very quick absorption of high quality nutrition which leads to an increased energy level of your body.

If weight loss is your ultimate goal with juicing then you must understand that by applying juicing as a weight loss solution is a very natural way of losing weight.

You must understand the fact that achieving weight loss through improved nutrition like juicing is one of the best benefits of juicing and if weight loss is your goal this fact alone should be very motivational for you. Take advantage of this side effect of juicing. I call this the effortless way of losing weight as opposed to going through some weird and complicated diets that are replacing some bad things that you should not eat anymore. Usually the latest and greatest fad diets tell you to replace the bad stuff with the good stuff but in a very unnatural and extreme way.

A diet in general does not work because it is too demanding, unrealistic and too extreme. I never succeeded in losing weight by following a diet because in the end I gained all the weight that I lost in a very unnatural and suppressing way. Juicing is the only natural way that I know of that gives the body all nutrients that it needs while still being able to lose weight because the weight loss kind of happens as a natural side effect and automatically.

Remember that juicing does remove the fiber so be sure to always include fiber rich food in your daily diet plan that you are following with your juicing for weight loss goals.

In my case, when I lost 40 lbs with juicing and smoothies I did not follow an extreme diet that in my opinion is just a waste of time.

I followed my daily juicing and smoothie ritual and followed a light and healthy fiber rich meal plan without following a particular complicated diet plan that some genius health guru figured out. I had lots of fibers, vegetables, protein like lean chicken and avoided food with fat and sugar. Instead of white bread, I opted for whole wheat, etc. without following any complicated diet plans or formulas that keep tricking the body into believing something that in the end leads to some catastrophic disaster. I consumed just natural, organic and lean food without fat and sugar in order to get enough fiber because the juices do not provide enough fiber.

If you are using juicing to lose weight, you really must understand that juicing should only be a complement to a well- balanced healthy and natural diet, not a substitute because this would again make it an unnatural and extreme process which is why most diets do not work!

As you can see juicing is a very natural process and the opposite of an extreme diet. If you follow these rules, you will soon discover that your body learns to function in a very effective and balanced way that helps you lose weight and keep your weight off effectively while keeping you satisfied;

Once you have achieved a metabolism that balances itself naturally while losing weight in the process and while being able to keep the weight off, you will understand the difference between a lifestyle with juicing which is a very natural process and a diet. By following a diet you have to respect some weird and complicated plan. With juicing you are living a lifestyle that I can call a happy, healthy, natural, balanced, satisfied, clean and lean eating lifestyle.

So as you can see with a little planning and creativity, the process of juicing can enhance your well-being, health and your well balanced diet which in turn helps you lose weight in an automatic and very natural way.

All the recipes that I have included in this juicing book are great for getting started with juicing for weight loss. These recipes helped me lose 40 lbs in 2 months and many of my family members and friends that have tried them out achieved similar results.

Go through them as you see fit and apply my tips for juicing for weight loss and you will find a great satisfaction and balance once you are done.

You will discover for yourself that juicing is very beneficial and that you want to keep the habit of juicing. This is how you will be able to live a lifestyle free of diseases and toxins. This is how you keep your body lean and clean. This is how you keep the doctor away. This is how you stay beautiful, keep balance, stay healthy and fit from the inside out and this is how you ultimately double your life!

Effortless Juicing Process

Preserve yourself from overeating by drinking a big cup of juices well before eating.

If you are able to pinpoint a juice extractor that is certainly high quality and operates on lower speeds, this would be your best choice. Increased speed might overheat your machine and thus destroy the nutrients of your juices.

Make sure to refer to the Green Star Juicer Review which has advantages as opposed to other juicers in relation to this overheating issue.

If you are in an age bracket over 50, you should be thinking to include juicing into your lifestyle in order to reduce the process of aging.

Pick a product or service which can be premium quality, simple to use and valued to match within your spending budget.

Add ginger to your juices and meal plan. Adding ginger to your juices also provides you with zesty flavor. Ginger also has a anti-inflammatory quality. It helps you recover injuries.

Purchase a masticating juice extractor which will keep the nutrition in the juices that you are making.

If you prefer juices without the pulp, I recommend to use an espresso filtration system or some cheesecloth to filter out the pulp.

Make sure to always include green super foods like kale, broccoli and spinach into your juices and shoot for 50%-75% plant based ingredients plus some other veggies and fruits for the sweet flavoring and to balance the sometimes bitter flavor of the veggies.

Should you be juicing as a result of health problems, make sure to get started with dark green fruits and leafy vegetables as your basic juices.

Never use industrial fruit juices to replace real fruits because they are full of natural sweets and consist of much less nutrients and vitamins than fresh juices.

If you do not like the bitter taste of some veggies make sure to balance the flavor with fruits like apples. In my opinion apples like Fuji, Rome, and Gala are the providing the best flavor.

When attempting to lose weight with juicing, try to create pineapple liquid with your juicer and you will find that adding apples are a wonderful combination with pineapple juice.

If you are on a juicing diet, you may want to lower the calories by adding an equal amount of ice cubes or source water.

Make time for yourself to truly enjoy your juices and try to get a feel for the different ingredients and flavors.

Juicing is even much easier and much more fun when the entire family takes part in the process. Have a child wash the fruits and veggies while a grown-up chops and processes it. If you include your kids, you will keep them interested and integrated into a healthy lifestyle at an early age which will benefit the health of your child enormously. Imagine not having to run to the doctor for every disease the child might come up with!

Make sure to respect the amounts and the combination with real healthy food because juicing alone is not a solution. It is always

meant in a way to substitute your healthy daily diet in order to keep you and your family fit based on the highly nutritious value that you will be supplied with from these healthy juices.

Make sure to research and know the benefits of the veggies and fruits that you are using. Every single vegetable and fruit gives distinct vitamins and nutrients and you must be aware what they do for you.

Improve your everyday intake of nutrients by making juicing part of your eating habits. Your whole body will reap the benefits plus you will find that these juices are not only healthy and fat burning in nature, but these juices are also super easy to make and taste deliciously.

Juicing is a simple to acquire skill and if you turn this skill into a habit, you will be able to live a clean, toxin free and lean life from the inside out and for a very long time.

Juicing keeps the doctor away and doubles your life!

Power Up Your Juicing Habits

Wheat grass is simply put a young wheat plant. Wheat grass is widely consumed in liquid form by health conscious people who prefer the concentrated rich source of enzymes, minerals and vitamins.

The main aspect that makes these wheat grass juices so healthy is the fact that it contains chlorophyll.

Nearly 70% of wheat grass is chlorophyll. Some individual state that a small pound of wheat grass is equal to 20 pounds of fresh garden greens! This is just one of the reason why health fans are liquefying this grass and drinking it.

Wheat grass juice is quickly rising to the top of the favorite juices.

It retains most of the essential minerals. These mineral enzymes and vitamins are promoting health and help repair cell damage.

Wheat grass juice also has the ability to increase oxygenation in the human body plus it helps build up the red blood cells. These red blood cells are the carriers of oxygen to the body's cells. In addition it purifies our blood and organs while destroying the nasty toxins. In general, wheat grass is a true metabolism booster.

Wheat grass juice is the perfect replacement for dark green leafy vegetables that you should supplement your diet with.

Wheatgrass is also a very rich source of alkalinity for the body. It is often found in supplemental form so that you can mix it with water and drink it if you do not have an adequate juicer that can process wheat grass. Some fans choose to drink a daily glass of fresh wheatgrass juice to insure that their body is getting enough alkaline forming food.

Juicers can break down the cellulose barriers and extract all of the juice inside fruits, grasses and veggies.

However, you should know that not all juicers are capable of making real wheat grass juice.

If you try to juice wheat grass in a juicer that is not made to process grass, you will probably end up with a damaged or clogged juicer.

The best juicers for wheat grass are those that are multipurpose juicers. These multipurpose juicers will not only make juices from veggies and fruits, but you can apply them to make wheat grass.

If you have any questions, simply ask lots of questions before buying your juicer.

You may want to purchase a wheat grass juicer if you plan to only process grass. These juicers are also known as single auger juicers. They are crushing the grass while squeezing out all of the rich chlorophyll juice of the grass.

Newer models of these single auger juicers do include two levels. The first level works to crush the grass and squeeze out the healthy juice while the second level pulls the remaining pulp through a second crushing and extraction process.

Today you can find many models of these auger or juice extractors. Do not let buying a juicer get in your way. Simply identify what type of juicer you want by determining what type of ingredients you want to process.

Remember, when you get into the habit of drinking healthy wheat grass juice, you should go step by step and start out slowly because the taste of the wheat juice might surprise you at first.

I did not like the taste at all when I got started, but learned how to integrate these healthy green juices into my daily juicing ritual.

I started by drinking one ounce per day and slowly work my way up to three ounces per day which is the perfect amount in order to get the most nutritious value into the system of the body.

You will see that such a habit will bring long term health and a lean and clean body!

Green Star Juicer Review

Staying healthy is something that is directly related to having good eating habits, an effective organization of your daily chores and a balanced lifestyle.

In my opinion it also entails a balanced food choice and diet plan that is rich in all types of nutrients. The right amount of nutrients is also important.

Juicers like the Green Star juicer have become extremely popular and important in modern society so that people can be able to balance their food choices in a healthier and more effective way.

However, the market for any kind of juicers these days is too large in order to make a smart choice from the get go and without being informed. Before you actually purchase any juicer, you should actually go through the benefits and features of the juicer that you consider.

In my view the Green Star Juicer is a good choice even though I prefer the Breville.

It is my duty to inform you about a second option that is available to you and that you might consider as a second choice if you do not want to go with the Breville.

The following is a list of items to expect with the purchase of a Green Star juicer.

Retractable Plug Green Star Juicer:

It is very likely that when you operate the machine without reading the instructions, you will not be able to find the plug.

This is a very common error because the plug and the wire extension of these Green Star Juicers do have their own designated place inside the juicer itself because the juicer has a retractable plug.

Solid Body Green Star Juicer:

The first thing you notice when you see or touch a Green Star juicer is that it is made to be of durable and stable materials.

It is based on a very balanced construction and everything is efficiently located and equated with this juicer.

Since juicers and similar products tend to be on the expensive side of things, it is very important that you take a look on the quality of the materials and the durability.

Heat Transfer Green Star Juicer:

The heat transfer from the machine to the juicer is a major issue with most juicers because heat transfer can destroy the nutrients in the veggies and fruits.

This juicer has a slow two-gear system. This system is critical and crucial to the quality of the juice.

You should really take a closer look before making your final decision because this juicer has some critical and obvious benefits.

Array of Attachments Green Star Juicer:

There are very important applications for the Green Star juicer in pasta making as well. If you are a pasta lover this is absolutely for you!

This is why taking a closer look at the Green Star Juicer if you are looking to buy a food processor at the same time.

This juicer is available in a wide array of attachments. This fact alone will increase the application of this juicer which in turn makes this option a very good solution in terms of the value that you are getting for your money.

Warranty Green Star Juicer:

Another big advantage of the Green Star juicer is that it comes with a five years attached warranties.

This means that if there is some kind of problem in this period then you can get it fixed without any problems.

Final Verdict For The Green Star Juicer:

A Green Star juicer is an extremely loaded machine that will not only improve the quality of life with regards to taste and quality of nutrition, but it also gives you a huge array of variety like making pasta and processing other types of food.

The 5 year warranty is yet another benefit that is almost unmatched by the industry and this is a real competitive advantage over the other products that only offer 1 year warranties.

Breville Speed Juice Extractor Review

Juicing is one of the most popular health trends at the moment. It detoxifies the body system. Juicing gives you a strong dose of nutrients and vitamins and minerals.

Juicing can even help you lose weight and maintain a healthy living. If you are interested in a juicing diet, I recommend a juice extractor. A juice extractor will be a helpful, usable and valuable addition to your daily food plan and lifestyle.

There is a big choice of juicers available and it can be a difficult process to determine which juicer is best for you.

In my view it is clear as day that the Breville BJE510XL Ikon Juicer is the best choice because it has consistently performed better and more effective than the competing juicers. The Breville is one of the best juice extractors on the market today.

Juicing Performance Of The Breville

You want to make sure that your juicer is able to extract juice from fruits and veggies without leaving much of excess pulp behind. The Breville BJE510XL will perform in this respect. It extracts only the optimal amount of nutritious juice from veggies and fruits.

Ikon Jucier Overview of The Breville:

900 watts
Measures 16 x 9 x 16 inches
5-speed system
Speeds range from 6500 rpm to 12500 rpm
Weighs 9 pounds

Volume Level Of The Breville:

The Breville seems to generate the same amount of noise as the competitors like the Green Star Juicer and others.

The noise will depend on your individual noice tolerance. You can expect it to make the same level of noise as an average juicer or blender.

Speed Of The Breville:

The Breville BJE510XL is designed with a speed control. The speed of the machine can be adapted to the veggies and fruits that are used. When you are juicing with the Breville, veggies and soft fruits do require a slower speed than firmer and crunchier fruits and veggies like broccoli. The Breville is designed with a control that allows you to effectively run the machine at exactly the right speed to get the most out of the juice.

It is designed to use the minimum effort to achieve the maximum results. The Breville also comes with a user-friendly manual. The manual tells you the exact speed that you should set for each ingredient.

This gives you the maximum output of juice and a minimum of messing around.

Juicer Design Of The Breville:
The Breville has a large shoot. It is spacious enough to fit several carrots or a whole apple in at a time. This reduces the time you can spend and it takes away the tedious tasks of slicing, dicing and chopping.

This juicer is something you are going to be proud to show off in your home. It has a very sleek and stainless steel finishing which will complement almost any home decor. The classy design earned a designer prize, the Australian Design Award.

Another feature of the Breville which contributes to the look is the fact that it will not stain after usage. Many juicers become discolored after usage, but the Breville BJE510XL is easy to clean and always returns into its original appearance after usage.

The Breville Juicer comes with several parts. It creates a firm seal when all the parts are snapped together. The juicer comes with a bright LCD screen. The LCD screen shows your current settings with fruit icons. This will guide you to select the matching speed for each ingredient.

What Comes With The Breville?
When you buy the Breville juicer you get a manual, a juice jug, a detachable spout, a froth separator and a cleaning brush.

Clean Up Of The Breville

Many consumers do love the Breville juicer because it is especially easy to clean up. When it is running, you will notice that all of the pulp is deposited into a separate container. If this seperate container is lined with plastic, it will quickly and easily be able to be emptied out. The various parts of the Breville juicer easily disassemble and fit easily into your dishwasher.

Warranty Of The Breville?

1 year of replacement warranty comes with the Breville BJE510XL juicer.

Juicing Quiz

All you have to do is find 12 Juicing Ingredient related words. Use your imagination, read backwards, sideways, and forwards to find the correct Smoothie related words and associations. Go to the next page to see the correct answers!

Have fun:)

Answers

Quiz Answers:
1. Orange
2. Apple
3. Lime
4. Ginger
5. Kale
6. Celery
7. Carrots
8. Beets
9. Strawberries
10. Spinach
11. Parsley
12. Fennel

Conclusion

I have a lot of fun experimenting with these juicing recipes and I hope that these same recipes are getting you started with your own juicing goals, too.

There's a lot of satisfaction when you stumble on a healthy juicing recipe that tastes fantastic. It's more gratifying if the recipe is 5 minute simple to make and if it is helping you shed pounds at the same time.

Don't be afraid to add or remove ingredients to make the recipe your own and as Ann Wigmore, one of the front-runners of today's raw food movement, declared, "Be creative; you just need to understand approximately what to do."

When you do make changes, jot them down! There is little worse than playing around and making a great recipe only to realize you can't remember precisely what you probably did. By making juices that you adore, you'll find yourself anticipating your juice breakfast or juice break.

Since they're so high in nourishment, you will begin to feel more fit.

If you're like me, you may also find that the more that you drink juices for weight loss, the more that you will begin to enjoy healthier food options like salads and fresh items. Convenience foods like potato chips will begin to taste tasteless.

The additional energy you get from the fruit, vegetable and plant based juices will also assist you in working out more.

All this mixed will assist in making your dieting efforts a big success!

I attempted to make this Juicing weight management system as easy, fascinating, inspiring, easy to use and as practical to consume as possible for you because a system like this has to be compatible with today's moving and mobile world.

Just keep the book on your portable gadget next to your working table and go through one recipe at a time and as you progress with your weight reduction challenge.

The book is intended to be used in an interactive and stimulating fashion and to empower you to take action at the same time.

Remember the juices are 5 minute quick to prepare so this even works for the busiest person in the world.

Ultimately, the goal of this book is to lead you to a healthy lifestyle that includes healthy and nutritious juices and food choices.

You can start with a Juicing diet first. Once you have shed the pounds and are satisfied with your weight loss it is important to keep off the pounds.

Including these healthy juicing drinks into your daily meal plans and including them into your lifestyle is what you should be aiming for as your ultimate goal, too.

Once you are at the level of including healthy juices into your daily lifestyle and once you are successful with keeping and maintaining your weight by choosing healthy food choices like these juice drinks, you have achieved your ultimate dieting goal!

This is a goal that you will never be able to achieve with an extreme and unhealthy diet because once the diet is over you'll regain weight and you'll be starting yet another fashionable diet again. This is a plan for error and disaster and it is called the Yo-Yo effect.

The plan of the Juicing diet, however, is very kind and intelligent because it follows the rules of the body. It nourishes and energizes the body throughout the day with all the beneficial ingredients and nutrients that are beneficial for the body and mind and it keeps your body and mind productive all the time.

I have explained to you the difference between a Juicing diet and the latest and greatest diet inside the chapter called Juicing For Weight Loss.

I hope you will use and consume the content whenever you need some inspiration and motivation for making some healthy Juice drinks that are either helping you with your weight loss goal or that you just like to include into your daily meal plan because you are already living the healthy lifestyle.

Remember, all you have to do is open the book and start with the first juice drink preparation.

Go through all of them and apply them on a daily basis as you see fit and depending on the health or weight loss goals that you are looking to achieve.

If you are a beginner with juicing, get started with the Powerful Beginner's Juice and go from there.

You will soon see for yourself that making these juices is a lot of fun plus a lifestyle with juices is going to make you very happy, satisfied, balanced, fit, lean and clean.

To your success with Juicing!

Did you love *Fasting Book For Health, Fitness, Weight Loss & Detoxing 11 Juicing For Beginners Recipes With delicious & Healthy Fruit & Vegetable Juices*? Then you should read *Blender Cookbook: 60 Blender Cocktails Recipes For Body Cleanse & Detox, Energy, Vitality & Rapid Weight Loss* by Juliana Baltimoore!

Blender Cookbook: 60 Blender Cocktails Recipes For Body Cleanse & Detox, Energy, Vitality & Rapid Weight Loss...Why Juice Fasting & Smoothies for Weight Loss Works? Here is the thing. Know about the know the specific ingredients that will help you meet your the body's and mind's nutritional needs. The trick here is to chose those ingredients that do not promote fat building up inside of your body. You know yourself and by applying common sense that fad diets as a solution to weight loss is not a solution at all. Diet trends never last over a long period of time and it is just a matter of time to see people who still believe in these diets go from one diet to the next one. This is a sad vicious circle which will never end. The healthier and more realistic alternative to this sad scenario is more of a lifestyle than a diet and it is called fast juicing + the smoothie diet lifestyle. What is great about drinking juices and smoothies is the fact that it is the perfect weight loss solution for females and males. It is the perfect lifestyle for working moms, busy people, people who are on the go, travellers, workaholics, lazy people, young and old. It is perfect for people who are looking for a quick and easy solution that is healthy, delicious and quick and easy to fix. The juicing and smoothie lifestyle is perfect for today's busy people because it does not take lots of time out of the day. Guess what 5 effortless minutes is all it is going to take you. So what do you need to get started? All you really need to get started with this exciting juicing & smoothie lifestyle is an instructional juicing and smoothie book that provides you with the recipes that you need to consume in order to get started, some kitchen supplies like a blender and a juicer (a high quality & high speed stand alone kitchen aid like the breville juicer and the nutribullet work best), a glass of fresh source water, your favorite cutting knive, and a cutting board is all you really need. To get you started with these powerful and beneficial blender recipes and juice fasting recipes right now here is what you will find inside: * Easy & Quick To Make Smoothie & Juicing Recipes For Effortless & Long Term Weight Loss Results * Clean Green, Vegetable & Fruit Pound Dropping Smoothie & Juicing Recipes * Cleansing Juicing Recipes & Smoothie Recipes For Weight Loss * Juice Fasting Detox Recipes & Smoothie Detox Recipes For Weight Loss You will also get Simple, easy & scrumptious recipes for: * Low-carb Smoothies & Juices That Will Help You Drop The Pounds And Keep Them Off Your Body * Powerful Immune System Booster Blender Recipes That Maximize Your Results * Fast Juicing & Powerful Smoothie Diet Recipes For Body Detoxification & Healing Of course a light Workout or body-building program is recommended in combination with this Juice Fasting & Smoothie Diet lifestyle so that you will maximize all the health and weight loss benefits that come out of it. This book compiles the most scrumptious and health beneficial juicing a smoothie recipes for weight loss in one single compilation. Apart from simply providing you with a collection of recipes, you will also receive interesting facts and information about how to maximize your lifestyle with respecting the simple but effective rules of juice fasting and a smoothie diet. You will learn about some amazingly interesting knowledge about juicing cleanse and juicing detox that will boost your body and brain and maximize your health and well being. You will experience yourself that this is not going to be a traditional fad diet that does not work, but a total body and brain transformation with the pound dropping results. You will see how this transformation will also relate to all the other aspects of your life as a powerful side effect.

Take on this lifestyle challenge and make juicing and smoothies part of your daily routine...

Also by Juliana Baltimoore

Meditation Book For Beginners: 15 Daily Strength Training & Home Workout Yoga Routines For Beginning Yogi Students

Daily Meditation Beginner's Guide From Happines & Good Life to Stress Release, Relaxation, Healing, Weight Loss & Zen

Daily Yoga Routine Beginner's Guide For Happiness The Mindful & Healthy Lifestyle With Zen & Spiritual Eternity

Daily Meditation Eternity Prayer Poem Book For Positve Mindset, Motivation, Happiness, Success, Health & Relationships

Superfoods Recipes: Chicken Soup Recipes For Cold Recovery, Healthy Chicken Noodle Soup Recipes, Holistic Healing Chicken Recipes & Homemade Healing Noodle Soup With Chicken

31 Blender & Mixer Smoothie Recipes For Rapid Weight Loss

The Poetry Book For The Paleo Lifestyle

21 Green Fruit And Vegetable Smoothie Snacks: Green Fruit Yogurt Smoothies, Vegan Desserts & Herbal Veggie Bullet Blender Drinks

Blender Cookbook: 60 Blender Cocktails Recipes For Body Cleanse & Detox, Energy, Vitality & Rapid Weight Loss

Fasting Book For Health, Fitness, Weight Loss & Detoxing 11 Juicing For Beginners Recipes With delicious & Healthy Fruit & Vegetable Juices

Juicing Recipes Book For Vitality, Energy, Health And Fitness Nutrition 14 Healthy Clean Eating & Drinking Juice Cleanse Recipes

Smoothie Recipe Book To Gain Energy & Detox 17 Smoothie Bowl Recipes, Cleanse Drinks & Blender Mix Recipes To Feel Stronger

Fitness Cookbook: 60 Healthy Nutrition Blender Recipes, Vegan Gourmet Recipes, Juicing Drinks, Dessert Recipes & Healthy Ice Creams For Wellness, Health & Happiness

Juicing Recipe Book: 27 Epic Juice & Blender Recipes For Health, Detox, Weight Loss, Energy, Strength & Vitality

Scrumptious Paleo Desserts: Low Fat Low Cholesterol Dessert Recipes For A Healthy, Happy, Lean & Clean Eating Lifestyle

Weight Loss Juicing Recipe Book: Epic Juicer Mixer Blender Recipes For Loosing Body Fat, Body Cleansing & Detox

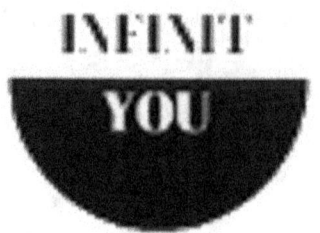

About the Publisher

InfinitYou is a hybrid general interest trade publisher. One of the first of its kind InfinitYou publishes physical books, electronic books, and audiobooks in various genres. Our publications are meant to educate, edify and entertain readers of all walks of life from babies to the elderly. Home to more than twenty imprints such as Infinit Baby, Infinit Kids, Infinit Girl, Infinit Boy, Infinit Coloring, Infinit Swear Words, Infinit Activities, Infinit Productivity, Infinit Cat, Infinit Dog, Infinit Love, Infinit Family, Infinit Survival, Infinit Health, Infinit Beauty, Infinit Spirituality, Infinit Lifestyle, Infinit Wealth, Infinit Romance, and lots more.

www.ingramcontent.com/pod-product-compliance
Lightning Source LLC
LaVergne TN
LVHW012127070526
838202LV00056B/5900